SO YOU WANT TO GROW A PIZZA?

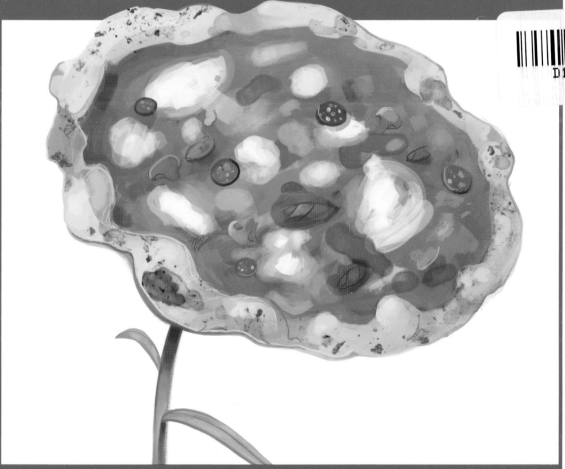

BY BRIDGET HEOS • ILLUSTRATED BY DANIELE FABBRI

AMICUS ILLUSTRATED • AMICUS INK

Amicus Illustrated and Amicus Ink
are imprints of Amicus
P.O. Box 1329
Mankato, MN 56002

Library of Congress Cataloging-in-Publication Data
Heos, Bridget, author.
 So you want to grow a pizza? / by Bridget Heos ;
illustrated by Daniele Fabbri.
     pages cm. — (Grow your food)
 Summary: "A young boy wants to grow his own
pizza, learns where the many ingredients come
from, and learns how to grow the ingredients to
make pizza sauce. Includes kid-friendly pizza sauce
recipe"—Provided by publisher.
 ISBN 978-1-60753-740-3 (library binding)
 ISBN 978-1-60753-907-0 (ebook)
 ISBN 978-1-68152-013-1 (paperback)
 1. Gardening—Juvenile literature. 2. Tomato sauces—
Juvenile literature. 3. Food—Juvenile literature. I.
Fabbri, Daniele, 1978- illustrator. II. Title. III. Series:
Heos, Bridget. Grow your food.
 SB457.H45 2016
 635—dc23   2014037339

Editor: Rebecca Glaser
Designer: Kathleen Petelinsek

Printed in the United States of America at
Corporate Graphics in North Mankato, Minnesota.

HC 10 9 8 7 6 5 4 3 2 1
PB 10 9 8 7 6 5 4 3 2 1

ABOUT THE AUTHOR

Bridget Heos is the author of more than 70
books for children including *Mustache Baby*
and *Mustache Baby Meets His Match*. She
has had a garden since fifth grade and is
currently growing tomato sauce and pumpkin
and cherry pie. You can find out more about
her at www.authorbridgetheos.com.

ABOUT THE ILLUSTRATOR

Daniele Fabbri was born in Ravenna, Italy, in
1978. He graduated from Istituto Europeo di
Design in Milan, Italy, and started his career
as a cartoon animator, storyboarder, and
background designer for animated series.
He has worked as a freelance illustrator
since 2003, collaborating with international
publishers and advertising agencies.

Pizza is delicious. Have you ever wondered where it comes from? Like all food, it comes from plants and animals. How would you like to grow a pizza at home?

You can't grow a whole pizza, of course.

But you can grow the ingredients.

The crust is made from wheat.
For that, you'll need a wheat field.

And for the cheese, you'll need milk.
That comes from a cow.

Do you like pepperoni? That's made from pork, which comes from a pig.

Uh-oh. Unless you live on a farm, you might be running out of space. Maybe you should start simple: grow the sauce.

Pizza sauce is made with tomatoes, garlic, and oregano. These plants need food of their own to grow. Plant food includes water, sunlight, and nutrients, which come from the soil.

Choose a sunny spot. Then add soil. You can make your own soil from compost. Compost is a mixture of stuff that used to grow as plants.

Keep the compost damp and turn it every few days. Soon, worms will move in. They'll eat the compost and turn it into soil. This will take a couple months!

Now it's time to plant. Garlic likes cold weather. Plant it in late fall. Pull the cloves of the garlic bulb apart. Plant them each in a small hole, pointy side up.

Your garlic will grow through the winter. But wait until late spring to plant your tomatoes and oregano. Otherwise, they'll freeze.

In spring, dig holes for the tomato plants. Place the plants, roots down, in the holes. Cover the bases with soil. Put metal cages around the young tomato plants. That way, the plants will grow tall and straight, not wild and crazy.

Next, plant the oregano. Make a line in the soil. Sprinkle the seeds along the line. Cover them with soil.

Water the garden. And wait. You can't see it, but your plants are growing . . . slowly.

When the oregano seeds sprout, they'll be a little crowded. Pull some so that others have room to grow.

Keep watering every few days if it doesn't rain. Also pull up weeds. If you don't, they'll steal food from your plants.

Soon it will be harvest time. When the garlic leaves turn yellow, carefully pull up the bulbs. Pick the red tomatoes off the vine. Cut some sprigs of oregano.

Now you can make the sauce and bake your pizza. And invite your friends over for a pizza party—with the freshest pizza sauce in town!

HOMEGROWN PIZZA SAUCE

INGREDIENTS

- 3-4 medium size tomatoes
- 2 Tablespoons (30 mL) olive oil
- 2 cloves garlic (Note, fresh garlic cloves should be hung up to dry for a couple weeks before using.)
- 3 Tablespoons (45 mL) chopped oregano
- Salt to taste

WHAT YOU DO

1. Have an adult help you peel and chop the tomatoes. (For a smoother sauce, put the tomatoes in the blender for several seconds.)
2. Chop the garlic cloves. In a large pot, simmer the garlic in olive oil until it is golden brown.
3. Add the tomatoes and oregano. Simmer at medium heat for 30 to 60 minutes, stirring occasionally. Add salt to taste. The sauce is ready when it is thick enough to be pizza sauce.

GLOSSARY

compost A mixture of dead plants that eventually becomes soil.

harvest To pick vegetables, fruit, or other plants that are ready to be eaten.

sprig A small branch with leaves or flowers.

sprout To grow and push up from underground.

READ MORE

Kuskowski, Alex. **Super Simple Kitchen Gardens: A Kid's Guide to Gardening**. Minneapolis: ABDO Publishing Co., 2015.

Sullivan, Jaclyn. **What's in Your Pizza?** New York: PowerKids Press, 2012.

Zoehfeld, Kathleen Weidner. **Secrets of the Garden: Food Chains and the Food Web in Our Backyard**. New York: Knopf, 2012.

WEBSITES

Kids' Farm: How Does Pizza Grow?
http://nationalzoo.si.edu/animals/kidsfarm/PizzaGarden/
Read about all of the plants and animals it takes to make what you need for pizza.

KidsGardening: Helping Young Minds Grow
http://www.kidsgardening.org/
The National Gardening Association has tips on how to start a garden at home or at school.

My First Garden: A Children's Guide
http://urbanext.illinois.edu/firstgarden/
Learn about the world of fun and clever gardening with step-by-step information on how to start a garden.

Every effort has been made to ensure that these websites are appropriate for children. However, because of the nature of the Internet, it is impossible to guarantee that these sites will remain active indefinitely or that their contents will not be altered.